How to make money selling apps

Ian Naylor

Copyright © 2017 Ian Naylor

All rights reserved.

ISBN-10:1544839545
ISBN-13: 978-1544839547

CONTENTS

1.	Introduction	pg. 4
2.	Choose a differentiator	pg. 5
3.	Build a website	pg. 7
4.	Set up your marketing	pg. 11
	i. Search Engine Optimisation	pg. 12
	ii. Content marketing	pg. 14
	iii. Social media	pg. 17
	iv. Paid marketing	pg. 18
5.	Sales	pg. 20
	i. Lead nurturing through email	pg. 21
	ii. Phone calls	pg. 23
	iii. Face to face meetings	pg. 25
6.	Post sales support	pg. 27
7.	Long-term marketing	pg. 29
8.	Conclusion	pg. 34
9.	About the author	pg. 35

1 INTRODUCTION

Small businesses have – in the past – been weary about launching a dedicated mobile app. High costs, and the technical skill required, contributed to this weariness, with a 2016 survey suggesting that only 20% of small businesses currently have a mobile app. But costs have fallen dramatically, and apps can now be launched with considerably more ease, creating a sizeable market for anyone in the business of selling apps.

With dedication, and a good structure in place, it is possible for entrepreneurs in this space to begin generating a six-figure income within 24-months. In this article, we will take you through the steps to follow in getting started, and putting the required structure in place. And when combined with your dedication, and AppInstitute's White Label App Reseller **Programme**, you will soon be on your way to generating a recurring revenue stream, and moving toward making a six-figure income just through selling apps.

2 CHOOSE A DIFFERENTIATOR

Competition is unavoidable; even businesses that start out as completely unique in the market soon find themselves with competitors. And going into business selling mobile apps will see you up against stiff competition. This is not a valid deterrent. It is an opportunity for you to set yourself apart, to identify what makes you and your business different, and to use that when promoting your business and services.

Start by identifying up to five local app development services in your area, and if there aren't any, then expand the area you are looking in. Now make a list of the services they offer, relating to app development for businesses. Look at the following:

- Do they offer different packages, and if so, what does each include?
- What is their pricing structure?
- What features do they offer with their product(s)?
- Do they offer any form of after-sales support?

Compare this to your own product, pricing, etc. and highlight where you are different. Rank them according to how much of a positive benefit they are to your potential customers. The one that offers the most benefit to your customers is your differentiator. The three most important factors to consider when evaluating your differentiator are:

- **Is it true?** Don't make anything up, and don't resort to negative marketing by lying about your competitors.
- **Is it provable?** This leads on from the first point; your differentiator must be demonstrably true.
- **Is it valuable to potential clients?**

Price is not a differentiator, and if there is no way to differentiate yourself from your competitors on features or service, do it by focusing on businesses of a certain size, or within a certain industry. Target only restaurants and caterers, or event planners. Or only target businesses with fewer than 10 employees. There is always a way to stand out, to be different.

Once you have established your differentiator, it should feature prominently in all your promotional material and in your sales pitches. It is what sets you apart, and it will allow you to stand out among your competition.

3 BUILD A WEBSITE

There is little reason for any business in the 21st century not to have a website, but it is unthinkable for any business promoting a digital product or service to not have a website. Modern website builder platforms make it easy – and affordable – for anyone to design and host a professional looking website. Unless you are quite comfortable designing and hosting your own website, you could consider any of the following:

WordPress – More than 27% of all current websites use the WordPress content management system (CMS). But in addition to the CMS, WordPress also offers a website builder, with hosting. From $8.25 per month, you get your own domain, access to hundreds of website templates, and the ability to customise your website. Note that with WordPress some knowledge of HTML and CSS will help.

Squarespace – Another all-in-one website builder platform, Squarespace offers a large number of templates that can be fully customized. Like WordPress, some knowledge of HTML and CSS will help, and pricing is from $12 per month, with your own domain included.

Strikingly – Strikingly is focused on helping you build and host a one-page website, with 11 templates to start off with, and the ability to add and remove sections. They have two paid packages available, with the higher priced ($16 /month) allowing more customization, and the ability to remove Strikingly branding.

Wix – Wix also offers many templates to help get you started, with the emphasis on drag-n-drop to customize your website. Pricing is from $8.50 per month, including your domain.

Whether you decide to host and design your website yourself or use a website builder platform, it is important that your website looks professional, and be accessible on mobile devices. Aside from that, your website should include the following:

> ➢ **Your offer** – details of the services you provide should be one of the first things a visitor to your website sees. Highlight important information and features in short paragraphs, linking to other sections of your website for more detailed information.

- **An 'About' section** – this is like a digital introduction, so should include a little bit about your background (and that of any other employees you have), along with relevant information about the company itself.
- **Pricing** – nobody wants to hunt for pricing information, or worse yet, contact you, so make sure this is easy to find. If you have a tiered pricing structure, list the features for each tier, and highlight what is unique about each tier.
- **Examples and Customer Testimonials** – this isn't possible when you're starting out, but you should plan for it. Examples are a nice visualization of what customers can expect, while testimonials help establish trust.
- **Contact Information** – like your pricing, you don't want potential customers to have to hunt for your contact information. At the very least you should list a telephone number, email address, and links to your company's social media profiles. List a business address only if you have an office that is always open during standard business hours.
- **Lead Capture Form** – Although your website includes your contact information, you should still have a lead capture form and call-to-action (CTA) setup. Use GetSiteControl, SumoMe, or Hello Bar to capture email addresses. and send them straight to your mailing list on most email marketing

platforms. They all offer free plans, with customizable email capture forms. Once your website starts attracting visitors, start testing different calls-to-action on your lead capture form. The most commonly used CTA for lead capture purposes is Signup, or Subscribe, but you may find better conversions using Learn More, See how it works, and other variations.

4 SET UP YOUR MARKETING

It is difficult, in an article this broad, to address all the aspects of marketing you should be taking care of, so instead, we will look at the basics that you can then build on.

(4) I. SEARCH ENGINE OPTIMISATION

Search Engine Optimisation (SEO) is an important marketing tool for any business with an online presence. But SEO is not only about peppering your content with appropriate keywords, it is also about attracting links, and being visible for local queries.

Start by adding your new business to Google My Business, and filling in as much detail as possible. Even broad queries are starting to bring in local results, so you could end up benefiting even more from this.

Attracting backlinks from other websites requires more effort, but will be easier once you build up a good catalog of content (see Content Marketing). In the beginning, you may want to:

- Ask your clients to add a link to your site on their website,
- Identify and then contact influencers in your industry, via social media and blogs,
- Get your business listed on relevant local online directories

The keyword element of SEO has also changed over the years. Our fractured search queries of the past have shifted to more semantic queries, so while individual words and phrases are still important, it is also essential to look at the inclusion of long-tail keywords.

Identify suitable keywords by using tools such as the Google Keyword Planner (free), Keyword Tool (free with limited options, Pro from $48/month), or Moz Pro (from $99/month).

It is important that you identify keywords and phrases that your potential customers would use in search. To help with that, and with building up a collection of long-tail keywords, try the excellent Answer the Public. All these tools allow you to filter your results, or customize the query by the search engine, or country.

Having a good understanding of which keywords your potential customers use is not only important for general SEO, but also for paid marketing, which we will cover later.

(4) II. CONTENT MARKETING

Google considers around 200 factors when determining a website's rank on search engine result pages (SERP). Two of those factors are the recency of content updates and the usefulness or quality of the content. And content marketing is about marketing your business by frequently sharing useful content with your audience. When done right, content marketing not only boosts your businesses visibility in search results but also helps establish you as a trustworthy authority within your industry.

Great content not only answers your customer's questions before they have asked them, it also – without asking – encourages them to share it, bringing your business additional exposure with minimal effort. But without a strategy, your content marketing will be a miss, rather than a hit. The simplest way to draw up a basic content marketing strategy is by answering these questions:

- **Who are your customers?** Create personas of your current and your target customers. You don't need to flesh them out in great detail, but enough for you to be able to describe them in one sentence.
- **Who are your competitors?** Look at both direct and indirect competitors, anyone who could draw customers (and

business) away from you.

- **What makes you unique?** Remember your differentiator? How can you incorporate that into your content, either in tone, or topics covered?
- **What are the problems your customers are facing?** This involves not only listening to what you customers talk about, but also what is being discussed online about their industries.
- **What do you want to achieve with your content?** Generally speaking, you want your content to drive sales, grow search traffic, build authority, and generate leads. But not all at once. Each piece of content you publish will influence one of those factors, and you just need to remain alerted so that you don't end up influencing one factor only.
- **How often will you publish new content?** It isn't feasible for any small business to try and publish new content on a daily basis. Once a week, or even once every two weeks is more manageable in the beginning. As your business grows, so too can your publishing schedule.
- **Where will you publish your content?** Obviously, you first publish on your website, but to assist in reaching an audience outside of your website, you should also share it on Twitter, Facebook, and any other social platforms used by your target audience.

➢ **Who will produce your content?** You? Not a problem if you are a good writer, and you have the time. But wouldn't your time be better spent pitching to actual clients? Consider using a freelance content writer instead. There is no commitment in terms of how often you use them, they are more affordable than you imagine, and they are no longer that hard to find.

➢ **How will you measure the results?** Your content marketing is not a failure if it isn't generating leads, increasing sales, bringing in more search traffic, etc. It means you have not been paying attention to which content does work. You need to track the results of each piece of content to identify what your customers respond to, and what generates the results you want. Establish how you will measure the results, and how those results will influence your content marketing strategy as a whole.

Remember that content marketing is not limited only to written articles. The content you 'publish' can also take the form of infographics, short video's, how-to guides, and even simple lists.

(4) III. SOCIAL MEDIA

Remember when we said it was unthinkable for any business promoting a digital product or service to not have a website? Well, the same applies to having a social media presence. There are 15 social media platforms attracting more than 15-million unique visitors each month, but you don't need to be active on all of them.

You only need to be active on those used by your target audience. Where possible, use the same username on all platforms, and this should also match your business name. Fill out the profile for each in full – don't skimp on any information – and try using your company logo as the profile photo.

Just as you created a strategy for your content marketing, you should create a strategy for your social media presence. Use the same questions as before, but remember that social media is not only for sharing content but also for engaging with your audience. And for capturing leads. Your strategy should also take into account what processes you are going to put in place to ensure you respond to any customer queries and comments on social media, on time. It should also cover which networks you are going to be active on and whether you are going to advertise on any of them.

(4) IV. PAID MARKETING

It is foolish to think that you can market your business without spending a cent. Paid marketing helps make you more visible to customers searching for businesses like yours, it helps you stand out amongst your competition, and it helps to keep you top-of-mind in potential customers who aren't yet ready to convert.

Paid marketing used to be limited to search engine marketing (SEM) and banner ads, but it now includes paid ads on social media. Aside from social media ads, most ads are charged on a pay-per-click (PPC) or cost-per-click (CPC) basis. CPC varies somewhat according to industry, and the keywords/phrases you are targeting. But it remains quite accessible to small businesses, with the right approach.

The key to running successful – and affordable – PPC/CPC and social media campaigns is to pay careful attention to your targeting. In most instances, you are trying to reach a smaller, more localized audience. After identifying the brand specific words and long-tail keywords you want to target in SEM, you then need to decide on the geographical location you want to target. You can then narrow your targeting further by looking at what times your target audience is most active, and what devices they use.

Although your advertising on social media is different to SEM and banner ads, the targeting options are not much different, and you should definitely use them.

Finally, there are many ways of analyzing the results of your campaigns, but the most important metric is your cost-per-acquisition (CPA) – how much do you spend on advertising to land one sale.

5 SALES

Leads are not sales, so although your website is setup to capture leads, you still need to nurture them through to a sale. But not every potential customer is going to visit your website or see your digital marketing. So we rely on three methods to generate and nurture leads, and close sales:

- Lead nurturing email campaigns
- Phone calls
- Face-to-face meetings

The goal of your email campaign should always be to convert a lead into a new customer, while you should use phone calls as a route to setting up a meeting.

(5) 1. LEAD NURTURING THROUGH EMAIL

Your website, as discussed earlier, gives potential customers an opportunity to learn more about your services. It also makes it possible for them to express interest by giving you their email address, which should then trigger your automated lead nurturing campaign. The campaign should consist of the following:

- 3-4 emails sent out over a period of 2-3 weeks.
- 1-2 campaign-specific landing pages.

Structure your email campaign to first welcome the customer with a brief introduction. The messages that follow should be educational, informative, and include a CTA that links to a specific landing page.

Use services such as Unbounce, Leadpages, or Instapage to create your landing page. They not only make it easy to design effective landing pages but also to split testing, allowing you to test pages with different layouts and text, to see which leads to the most conversions.

The subject line of your email message is as important as the message itself. Points to consider include:

- ➢ Use action verbs, such as **Save, Start, Discover,** and **Learn.**
- ➢ Brevity. Your goal should be a subject line of 5-7 words.
- ➢ Make it sound human, and DON'T USE ALL CAPS.
- ➢ Try to incorporate an emotional appeal: curiosity, urgency, joy, or enthusiasm. But make sure that what the subject line teases or promises matches what the message delivers.

Once you start measuring the results of your campaign, you will be most interested in the click rates. Open rates are important – after all, you want recipients to open your email messages – but they mean very little if people are not clicking on your CTA. As with everything you measure, pay attention to what does and does not work, so you know what to keep using, and what to keep improving.

(5) II. PHONE CALLS

Very few people are naturally good at making phone calls, especially as part of a sales pitch. Preparation and practice help, along with a willingness to assess your own "performance" afterward, learning from any mistakes you make. You don't want to sound like you're reading from a script, or that you've rehearsed the call, but you want your call to have a sense of structure.

Open with a professional greeting – good morning, or good afternoon – before introducing yourself and your company. Not all products and services can be sold with a phone call, and your objective is to schedule a meeting by selling what your product will do for your potential client. Try framing the purpose of your call as a question,

> "If we can show you a way to retain more customers and attract new ones, would that be something of interest?"

thereby provoking interest. If the customer seems keen, steer the conversation towards scheduling a meeting. And once you have the opportunity to schedule a meeting, do so by giving the customer two options, rather than asking them when they would like to meet,

"Mr. Johnson, I can pop by your office at 2:15 p.m. today to discuss this further. Or would 9:45 a.m. tomorrow better suit your schedule?"

Regardless of whether you are able to schedule a meeting or not, end the call by thanking them for their time. And if you do manage to schedule a meeting, send a meeting request via your calendar immediately after ending the call.

(5) III. FACE TO FACE MEETINGS

If you're not quite used to with face-to-face meetings, they can be every bit as intimidating as making that first phone call. But again, preparation and practice help.

If you haven't already done some research on your potential client, and the industry they work in, now would be a perfect time. Some of the points you should address in your meeting include:

- What an app could do for their business.
- What unique benefits are key to them.
- How an app could improve their bottom line.

and the more you know about their business and industry, the more accurately you can state the above. Your research should also help you clarify this person's role in the business. For very small businesses, you will likely be meeting with the owner, who also makes all the decisions. But for larger businesses, your first meeting might be with someone who is part of the decision making process. And how you present to a problem owner differs from how you would present to a budget owner. Yours is a product that is easier to sell through a demonstration, so always have a demo app ready when meeting with clients. If you are able to customize it to include their own logo, etc. so much better. Don't be afraid to show them actual apps you have already launched, even if it is for their competitor. Your presentation should include all essential information while being as brief as possible. But be prepared to answer any questions the client has, even if they were already answered in the presentation.

Unless the client has already given a clear indication during the meeting, don't be afraid to end the meeting by asking for their business,

> "So, off the back of everything we have covered today, do you feel an App would help keep your existing clients loyal and attract new ones? Would you like to go ahead and I will have your app live within 30 days from today?"

and if they need more time to digest what you have presented, suggest a follow-up date and time. For successful sales:

- ➢ give a brief outline of what happens before the app goes live, and
- ➢ ask for the details of anyone you need to communicate with to get required information.
- ➢ Finally, there will be some objections, but in time you will become quite familiar with many of them, allowing you to prepare standard responses to them.

6 POST SALES SUPPORT

A good app developer's relationship with a client doesn't end once their app has been successfully launched. Each sale you close will need a fair amount of effort on your part, but it will all be for naught if your customers abandon you, and their app, within the first month or two. A good app developer retains customers by offering great post-sales support in the form of:

- Assisting clients with their app marketing
- Advice on how to increase downloads
- Training clients on how to use the platform to update content
- Advice on how to create and send push notifications
- Regular newsletter updates covering business tips, platform updates, and general app advice

Much of this can be worked into your content marketing strategy, with you publishing in-depth guides on these topics. This doesn't replace the need for occasional one-on-one meetings with clients, where you give personalized advice and training. But it will help establish trust with potential clients, while also setting you up as a subject-matter authority.

Compile a plan of what your post-sales support will entail. Your plan should include:

- How frequently you will personally follow-up with each client after their app has launched.
- What each follow-up will involve – will it address a specific topic, or will it be a general follow-up only?
- What training will be available to clients?
- What topics will also be covered by in-depth guides on your business website? Include proposed publishing dates, updating these to the actual URL once published.
- The schedule for your newsletters, along with proposed subjects for each newsletter.

The plan should be a working document that you update as necessary. It doesn't need to be distributed to clients, serving more as a reference document for you should your clients ask about post-sales support.

8 LONG-TERM MARKETING

Short-term marketing – in the form of paid advertising, special email marketing campaigns, referrals, and discounts – helps give short lived boosts to your sales, while keeping you top-of-mind in potential customers.

But it is your long-term marketing efforts that will contribute the most to the success of your business. While your short-term marketing is designed to bring in new clients, your long-term marketing not only brings in new clients, but helps keep existing clients. Your long-term marketing efforts should address the following:

SEO Management – This is an ongoing process, and a vital one in terms of making your business discoverable to new clients. Search engines are constantly adjusting their search algorithms to ensure they always return the most relevant results. At the same time, the way internet users search for information is evolving. What this means for you is that you need to be aware of significant changes affected by popular search engines, particularly Google, while also being aware of what words and phrases bring in the most traffic to your website. Key points to look at for website and SEO management are:

- **Know your audience** – knowing what topics interest your current and target audience will help you create content that attracts them, and then guides them along the sales funnel.
- **Know your competition** – when it comes to search, your aim should always be to outrank your competition. Not outranking them makes you less visible to potential clients. Use an SEO tracking tool – such as Moz – to compare how you rank against your competitors. You can then use this information to analyze the topics and content where they are outranking you, along with the strategies they are using to outrank you. Naturally, you should not ignore any areas where you are outranking them, and for good measure, include one or two similar businesses that are not direct competitors to you. This could help you discover new content and keyword ideas, greatly improving your visibility ahead of your actual competitors.
- **Constantly optimize your content** – knowing what topics interest your audience, and what keywords they are using when searching for those topics, put you in a position to always have the freshest, most relevant content. You don't need to constantly revisit – and reoptimize – your older content, but your new content should always take into

account new trends and keywords within your industry. But never allow yourself to resort to keyword stuffing. Regular and long-tail keywords should always appear naturally in all your content. And if you are targeting a specific geographical location, it won't hurt to include local keywords occasionally.

➢ **Measure your performance** – Moz is great not only for tracking your competitors ranking, but also for measuring your own performance, and helping you to identify opportunities. Knowing what works and what doesn't work helps you to make adjustments in good time before your ranking and visibility are affected too much. An extra benefit is that you can use some of the insights when creating new paid marketing campaigns.

Of course, you would much rather focus on closing sales than obsess over keywords and SEO, but while you should have no problem finding an agency or freelancer to manage this for you, it helps if you have some understanding of the principles and practices that drive SEO management.

Fresh Content – your content marketing strategy is a very important part of long-term marketing. One of the reasons the frequency of your content updates is included in your strategy is because content marketing is ongoing. It isn't something you start, and then allow to fizzle out, so trying to publish more frequently than you can manage is like setting yourself up for failure. Publishing only twice a month is still acceptable for small businesses, as long as the schedule is consistent and – more importantly – the content is always very topical and relevant to your audience, or offers very valuable advice that they can use immediately. Keep your audience engaged by sharing relevant content from other websites via your Facebook and Twitter account, and by punctuating your published content with an email newsletter.

The emphasis is always on quality over quantity, because valuable content not only keeps your existing customers happy, it also draws in new customers. But do remember that this is long-term marketing. Don't give up on content marketing because of the lack of immediate results, and once you do start seeing results, you need to adjust your content marketing strategy to focus on the type of content that generates the best results.

Set benchmarks – one way of looking at benchmarks is to think of them as rules for winning. You want your business to succeed. You want to achieve the benchmark stated in this article's headline. But the only way to do that is to set smaller benchmarks and to work hard at achieving each of them. Start by setting a small, realistic sales goal for each month, breaking this down further into a sales goal for each week. Once you start achieving your goal consistently, begin increasing it in order to keep pushing yourself to grow. At the same time, you should be benchmarking yourself against your competitors. While benchmarking your performance against them might not be realistic, you can benchmark your practices, especially marketing, against them, ensuring you don't lag behind them and your industry as a whole.

8 CONCLUSION

Success is never guaranteed, and it is impossible for one article to provide you with all the answers to creating a winning business. But it is possible to combine industry knowledge with actual case studies, to set out tried-and-tested methods for laying the foundation of a successful venture. These steps do not provide you with a shortcut to making a six-figure income selling apps, but they do provide you with a path to follow, with suggested actions for you to take. The willingness to explore each step further, and the eagerness to put in the required effort, is all up to you.

ABOUT THE AUTHOR

Ian Naylor is the founder and CEO of AppInstitute, a leading B2B SaaS platform enabling small and medium sized businesses to create and manage mobile apps without any coding or tech skills.

AppInstitute were recognised as one of the top 50 Creative Companies in England by Creative England and have been featured in leading tech blogs and publications such as Mashable, Forbes, The Next Web, Tech Radar, ZDNet and Android Authority.

A serial entrepreneur, technologist and innovator, Ian is an expert authority on mobile app trends, development and online marketing. He has worked the world over during the last 15 years, starting and running various internet and technology businesses and can often be found giving seminars on mobile trends, online marketing strategies, growth hacking and how he grew his business from zero to £7.5million in just 200 pitches.

Ian has been featured on the BBC, Channel 4, Infoworld, VentureFest, Business Insider and is a regular contributor to leading marketing communities GrowthHackers and Inbound.org, alongside publications including Search Engine People, Business 2 Community and Curatti.

www.ingramcontent.com/pod-product-compliance
Lightning Source LLC
Chambersburg PA
CBHW061234180526
45170CB00003B/1295

9781544839547